THE
AMP
IT
UP
FIELDBOOK

FRANK SLOOTMAN

Chairman and Former CEO of Snowflake, Inc.

THE AMP IT UP FIELDBOOK

A Guide for Leaders, Teams, and Facilitators

WILEY

Library of Congress Cataloging-in-Publication Data is Available:

ISBN 9781394245024 (Paperback)
ISBN 9781394245031 (ePub)
ISBN 9781394245048 (ePDF)

Cover Design: Wiley

SKY10070751_032424

Contents

Preface

The role of leadership is to drive performance to change the status quo. The most effective leaders are able to identify opportunities within their organizations and pursue them to attain exceptional outcomes. They amp it up.

When people ask me about my secret to success, they may be surprised that the explanation is so simple. Anyone can do it. Most organizations are underperforming, whether their people realize it or not. The secret to amping it up is finding the slack that naturally exists and eliminating it by setting bigger goals, a faster pace, and a higher intensity. It's about pushing the organization to perform at a much higher level and reaping the results of your amplified efforts.

If anybody can do this, then why do so many organizations remain complacent? In some cases, it's simply because it's hard. Change is always hard, and amping it up will push people beyond what they have grown comfortable with. As a leader, you may become unpopular. People who don't keep up will leave. But those are the trade-offs needed to make meaningful change. When you give up the good-enough mindset and amplify your expectations, you gain far more than you lose.

In other cases, organizations plod along with the status quo because they don't know how to get started. While the approach is simple, the execution is not. This fieldbook forms the bridge that can help you move from the concepts described in *Amp It Up* to implementation in your own organization.

HOW TO USE THE FIELDBOOK

If you've already read *Amp It Up*, you know that I focus on execution. That's because even the best strategy will fail if the execution is weak. The fieldbook benefits from this approach by focusing on practical ways to execute the recommendations from *Amp It Up*.

This fieldbook's activities will help you create a concrete path to executing the ideas and guidance in *Amp It Up*. Each chapter in this fieldbook corresponds to a chapter in the main book, so I recommend you read or revisit each chapter there before digging into these activities. Most of the exercises will help you figure out what steps you must take to realize the principles described in the chapter. By applying the concepts from the book to your own situation, you will understand what to do and how to do it. The questions in this fieldbook will lead you to develop a plan to make those changes a reality.

If you haven't amped it up before, you may need to prepare yourself for the magnitude of change you are pursuing. To this end, some of the exercises will help you shift your mindset, so you can be ready to make a major impact on your organization or team.

WHO THE FIELDBOOK IS FOR

This book is for leaders at every level. No matter where you are in your career or what kind of organization you are part of—startup, nonprofit, established firm, small business—you can be a leader.

Drivers Wanted

To use the terminology from the book, the people who will benefit most from these activities are *drivers*. Drivers are the people who are invested in solving problems and improving their organization. They get their satisfaction from making things happen and they bring much needed energy to their team. When they face an amped-up goal or daunting project, drivers say, "Let's do it!"

Your organization needs drivers. As you start to amp it up, people who are passengers—the ones who are happy with the status quo—will leave, and that's okay because passengers struggle in an amped-up environment. Drivers, by contrast, are the people who kick the culture into overdrive to support the massive changes that are necessary to fulfill your mission and can execute at ever-higher levels.

Regardless of their place in the hierarchy, drivers will see value in the activities here. Middle managers can use these activities to amp up their team's performance, and to collaborate with like-minded department heads to give shared initiatives a boost. People on a management track will benefit from shifting their thinking to explore new ways to solve problems and tighten the slack in their area of control. Entry-level employees can sharpen their ability to see beyond the boundaries of their current roles and make significant contributions to their teams. People at all levels can use the strategies, techniques, and activities here to chart a career path that supports their ambitions. After all, drivers are going places.

Hypergrowth Is Not Just for Startups

My career has been mostly in the tech sector, which is dominated by fast-paced startups and entrepreneurial ventures, but *Amp It Up* is for everyone. While startups' do-or-die culture can be an excellent environment for amping it up, other organizations can benefit just as much—if not more—from the activities in this fieldbook. The approach is broad enough that all kinds of organizations can use the activities to execute in a way that supports their mission. There is no reason to follow my precise footsteps, especially if they don't lead you to where you want to go. The examples and stories from my experience serve as a starting point, and the activities here can help you adapt them for your own organization.

Established companies often fall into patterns of incrementalism. Shareholders and executives tend to suffer from short-termism and risk aversion, looking to progress a tiny bit each quarter. Long term, this slow-but-steady approach often turns out to be a death sentence. Large, well-known companies that play it safe likely have many opportunities for tightening up slack and boosting performance, if they are motivated to set goals that would incentivize it.

This fieldbook can help drivers in these firms plot a plan for meaningful growth.

Although nonprofit organizations may not be motivated by profits, hypergrowth would allow them to speed toward initiatives, broaden their mission, and have a greater impact on whomever they serve. Consider what you could accomplish if you set fundraising goals that were 25% higher—and reached them.

GETTING STARTED

The activities in *The Amp It Up Fieldbook* are designed so you can begin right away with minimal friction. I recommend you start with Chapter 1 and complete each chapter sequentially. As you complete individual activities, be honest with yourself, but don't be content with the status quo. This book isn't intended to reinforce what you're already doing. It's to help you achieve far more, so open yourself to ideas and projects that feel difficult or challenging. That's the point.

Organizations can get the most out of *The Amp It Up Fieldbook* if leaders amp it up simultaneously. Not only can this have a snowball effect that gets people thinking bigger and bigger, but it also helps cross-functional teams and projects collaborate on how to cultivate hypergrowth. The principles and concepts of *Amp It Up* work best when they can flow through the organization's culture, inspiring people at every level.

My hope is that this fieldbook helps you discover how to amp it up and take hold of the hidden opportunities in your organization.

THE
AMP
IT
UP
FIELDBOOK

1

Introduction: The Power of Amping Up

Being a leader at a fast-growing organization is hugely challenging. Not only are you responsible for setting the direction of your company, but you are also accountable for inspiring your people to maximize their performance to reach your goals. Focused leadership can bring instant energy to an organization, revving up performance and motivating your employees. By tapping into dormant potential, you can rejuvenate the company even before more structural changes get going.

The following activities will help you orient yourself as a leader and prime your thinking about what your organization needs and deserves from you.

GET THE LAY OF THE LAND

Consider the challenges, rewards, and excitement that are part of your daily life as a leader. Now, imagine you have succeeded in amping up your organization. What specific accomplishments would you be most proud of? What difficulties would you have overcome? How would you prepare for what comes next?

_____

_____

_____

_____

_____

_____

_____

What do you hope to learn? How do you think it will help you get from where you are right now to where you imagine you could be after a successful scale?

_____

_____

_____

_____

_____

_____

_____

Now, take stock of the areas in your organization that you can amp up. Based on your metrics and your instincts, what areas seem dormant or slow moving? How can you amp up their performance?

_____

_____

_____

_____

_____

ORGANIZATIONAL SCAN

Answer the following questions to get a sense of the work that you will need to do.

What is one way you can raise your standards to energize your people?

_____

_____

What is one way you can better align your people and the organizational culture you are working to create?

_____

_____

If you were to sharpen your focus on your single most important priority, what would it be?

_____

_____

How can you set the pace to shorten timelines and bring more urgency to your workplace?

_____

_____

Consider your current strategy. How can you transform it to better support hypergrowth?

_____

_____

2

My Journey from Teenage Toilet Cleaner to Serial CEO

My approach to business has developed as I've evolved professionally. In *Amp It Up*, I reflect on key learning experiences throughout my career because every experience—both good and bad—has shaped my philosophy and helped me figure out what works and what doesn't. Your career and approach to leadership will be different from mine, so it's important to understand your path as you begin this shift in the way you work.

The following activities will help you reflect on the most impactful professional experiences you've had so far. In doing so, you will gain clarity about what kind of leader you will be and how you can best help your organization thrive.

CAREER HIGHLIGHTS

Start by reflecting on three points in your career when you and your team experienced a high level of success. For each one, summarize what happened, why it is meaningful to you, and what you learned.

1. _____

_____

_____

2. _____

_____

_____

3. _____

_____

_____

Consider your current role and organization. How can you translate what you learned from these experiences to be a better leader in your current role?

_____

_____

_____

_____

_____

_____

TOUGH TIMES

As we discuss in the book, leadership success is almost never linear. There are great victories and success along the way but there are also other less successful times. Reflect on three points in your career when you and your team experienced difficulty and failure. For each one, summarize what happened, how the experience changed you, and what you learned.

1. _____

_____

_____

2. _____

_____

_____

3. _____

_____

_____

Consider your current role and organization. How can you use what you have gleaned from your leadership journey to avoid similar experiences?

_____

_____

_____

_____

_____

_____

YOU AS A LEADER

What are your strengths as a leader?

_____

_____

_____

_____

_____

_____

What are your weaknesses as a leader?

_____

_____

_____

_____

_____

_____

What kind of leader do you strive to be? What strengths would you choose and how would you interact with people?

_____

_____

_____

_____

_____

_____

Name a leader or manager you worked with and admired. How did their leadership style and approach to business help them succeed? Briefly describe a situation you believe they handled particularly well.

_____

_____

_____

_____

_____

_____

3

Make Your Organization Mission Driven

A compelling sense of mission can give organizations motivation and elevate their performance. Simply put, a mission establishes what a company is trying to accomplish. In mission-driven organizations, management effectively communicates why companies exist and why they matter. It's surprising how many companies struggle to identify this. This is more difficult than it might seem, but companies that adopt a mission-driven mindset have a competitive advantage.

Now that you've done some initial thinking, you can put your mission to the test. Great missions have three characteristics:

1. Big, but not impossible
2. Clear
3. Not about money

Work through the following activities to identify, hone, and establish a mission that can drive your organization.

DRAFT YOUR MISSION

Think about what your organization does on a strategic level. What is its purpose? Why does it exist?

_____

_____

_____

_____

_____

_____

What is your role in accomplishing that mission?

_____

_____

_____

_____

_____

_____

Consider each of these attributes to strengthen the mission you created in the previous activity. We'll examine them one by one in the following sections.

BIG, BUT NOT IMPOSSIBLE

Some missions are too big to be meaningful, while others are too small to make an impact. Consider Snowflake's current mission:

> *To mobilize the world's data by building the world's greatest data and applications platform, not just of the cloud era, but in the history of computing.*

Let's break this down to see why it works.

Mission Statement Component	Why It Works
To mobilize the world's data	• This part of the mission focuses on who we serve. At Snowflake, our clients rely on data, and they come from every industry and around the globe. • This is big thinking, but being a global company is realistic.
by building the world's greatest data and applications platform	• This part focuses on what Snowflake does and produces, specifically a data and applications platform. • Since Snowflake's aim is to serve global customers, we need to develop a world-class platform.
not just of the cloud era, but in the history of computing	• This part of the mission keeps us oriented to the future. It gives our mission longevity so it can carry us beyond our immediate situation. • The idea of making a place for ourselves in history also keeps us ambitious.

Now, work with your draft mission to make sure it's big enough to be ambitious and focused enough to align with your company's purpose. Start by answering these fundamental questions:

1. Who do you serve? *Be specific enough to relate to your core business, but think big enough to reach as many people as you realistically can.*

_____

_____

2. What is your company's purpose, amped up? *Link this to your company's core business and strategy. Now, make it ambitious enough to inspire the people who work for you every day.*

_____

_____

3. What do you envision will be your company's legacy? *Consider how your company aims to change the world. Think about what your clients and industry will value your organization for. How will your team leave its mark long term?*

_____

_____

CLARIFY YOUR MISSION

A mission that is fuzzy, vague, or constantly changing cannot be effective. Now that you have an idea about the size of your mission, it's time to get as much clarity on that mission and your daily role in it as possible. The goal of this activity is to remove distractions so you can home in on what matters most.

Identify three powerful distractions. *Distractions are not necessarily unimportant. In fact, they are often compelling enough that they can steal your team's focus. Distractions can include workplace politics, fleeting industry trends, or wider ideals that your company is not prepared to address as part of your core business. Knowing what these are ahead of time will help you maintain your focus.*

1. _____

2. _____

3. _____

If any of these distractions are sneaking into your mission, adjust your aperture to force them out.

MEASURING YOUR MISSION

As you know by now, a good mission is not about money. If you bring good things into the world, rewards will follow. Consider the daily lives of your employees and customers. How does successfully pursuing your mission affect them? What three nonfinancial metrics can you measure to track your progress?

1. _____

2. _____

3. _____

LIVING THE MISSION EVERY DAY

The key to being a truly mission-driven organization is to live your mission every day. What are three ways you can support the mission as an individual? *Consider how you can draw on your mission when making decisions and executing important aspects of your job.*

1. _____

2. _____

3. _____

Now, consider your organization's culture. What are three things you can do to help your employees connect with the mission?

1. _____

2. _____

3. _____

Finally, how will you know your company lives the mission every day? What will that look like on a large and small scale?

1. _____

2. _____

3. _____

As a reminder that your organization's strategy is always adapting, Snowflake's mission statement has changed since *Amp It Up* was first published. Today, we've simplified it, so Snowflake's current mission is "to mobilize the world's data." We haven't given up on the rest of it, but that has become a part of our DNA, so it goes without saying.

4

Declare War on Your Competitors and on Incrementalism

The cold truth is that business is much more like war than most people would care to believe. Your competitors are trying to steal your customers and cut into your profits, so you need to play defense and offense at the same time. Having excellent products will only get you part of the way to success. You also need to cultivate allies within your customer organizations and entice talent away from your competitors. Perhaps even more important is declaring war on incrementalism to pursue audacious goals. One of the keys to defeating your competitors—especially longtime industry players—is a solid growth model that will help you push the limits of your business.

The following activities will help you prepare a battle plan for a war fought on two fronts: against your competitors and against incrementalism. They will also consider how you can best lead your people as you pursue your audacious goals together.

KNOW YOUR ENEMY

Knowing the enemy is a key part of your battle plan. Consider your biggest competitor and analyze their value proposition by first focusing on their strengths. What do they promise their customers? What do they do particularly well?

_____

_____

_____

_____

_____

Now, while remaining objective, identify their weaknesses. Instead of focusing on how your offering is better, describe all the potential pitfalls their customers could encounter and resist the urge to defend your company's position. Is anything about their business model unsustainable? What is most likely to disappoint customers? What trade-offs do customers make when they sign with your top competitor?

_____

_____

_____

_____

_____

Understanding your competition's strengths and weaknesses is critical to helping you play defense. It will also help you see openings for you to go on the offensive, but to do that, you need to take stock of your own organization.

KNOW YOURSELF

To develop a battle plan, you need to understand yourself at least as well as you know your enemy. What is your company's value proposition? What does your organization do particularly well?

_____

_____

_____

_____

_____

Now, keep an open mind and turn a critical eye on yourself. Your company might also struggle with some of the same issues your competitors face, but you might face a different set of challenges. Is anything about your model unsustainable? What are the top complaints you receive from customers? How do you struggle to compete in the industry?

_____

_____

_____

_____

_____

_____

In the following activities, we'll take a closer look at what your organization does well, what it could be doing better, and how those elements can come together to create an audacious goal.

BANISH INCREMENTALISM

The first battle in your war on incrementalism is locating it within your organization. Review your business goals for this year or quarter, then reflect on your market and industry. Could you double that goal? Could you quadruple it? Could you reach it if it were 10 times more ambitious?

Select three goals or objectives that you could replace with bold and audacious goals to transform your business and supercharge your performance. Write them down in the left column of the table provided here. Then, in the right column, write down the audacious goal you will pursue instead.

Incremental Goal/Objective	Audacious Goal
1.	1.
2.	2.
3.	3.

Once you have determined your audacious goals, you need a concrete plan to help you reach them. What outcomes do you need to achieve? Write them down here.

Audacious Goal 1: *What outcomes must you realize to reach this goal? What steps will you take to get there? What tools or people will you rely on? What resources will you need to replace incremental progress with hypergrowth? How will you measure your progress toward that goal?*

_____

_____

_____

_____

Audacious Goal 2: *What outcomes must you realize to reach this goal? What steps will you take to get there? What tools or people will you rely on? What resources will you need to replace incremental progress with hypergrowth? How will you measure your progress toward that goal?*

_____

_____

_____

_____

Audacious Goal 3: *What outcomes must you realize to reach this goal? What steps will you take to get there? What tools or people will you rely on? What resources will you need to replace incremental progress with hypergrowth? How will you measure your progress toward that goal?*

_____

_____

_____

_____

ADOPT A GROWTH MINDSET

You're about to go to war against the way most of the world does business, so you need to prepare yourself for real innovation and growth. One way to do that is to eliminate your fear or doubt by answering the following questions.

Imagine you reach all three audacious goals. *What did you gain? What did you sacrifice? What does your business look like?*

_____

_____

_____

_____

Envision achieving 50% of each goal. *What did you gain? What did you sacrifice? What does your business look like?*

_____

_____

_____

_____

Imagine you fail to make any progress on any of the three goals. This is unlikely, but imagine the worst possible outcome. *What did you gain? What did you sacrifice? What does your business look like? What did you learn about yourself and your organization? What changes do you need to make to improve your organization's performance?*

_____

_____

_____

_____

Keeping these answers in mind, complete the following by listing the risks and potential rewards of your war on incrementalism.

Risks	Potential Rewards

There is almost always more to be gained than to be lost. Spend some time reviewing this list. If you are uncomfortable with the risks and feel there isn't enough potential upside, revisit your audacious goals to find a better balance. Do not slip back into the trap of incrementalism. Reimagine your business and set goals that will support dramatic change.

OUTPACE YOUR COMPETITION WITH A GROWTH PLAN

In this fast-paced world, you can either play it safe by chasing incremental progress, or you can become a challenger with new ideas. Eventually an innovative challenger will emerge and revolutionize your industry. This activity will help you become that challenger.

Review your competitor's strengths and weaknesses, then review your own. What does this reveal about opportunities in your industry? Ask yourself the following questions: *If you and your competitor have common weaknesses, how can you eliminate them? If you have unique weaknesses, how can you change your business so they don't matter anymore? What can you offer your customers that no one else can?*

List the opportunities you see here.

Opportunity 1:

_____

_____

Opportunity 2:

_____

_____

Opportunity 3:

_____

_____

Imagine you need to create a drastically different business model to take advantage of these opportunities. What would that look like for each opportunity?

Opportunity 1 Business Model: _____

_____

Opportunity 2 Business Model: _____

_____

Opportunity 3 Business Model: _____

_____

LEADING YOUR TEAM INTO BATTLE

One of the benefits of being a mission-driven organization is that it can help every person working for you have clarity about their priorities and how their work supports the company's most important goal. Tying your mission to your audacious goals will help your people recognize their role in the battle plan.

Think back on your mission statement from Chapter 3. How can you better fulfill your mission through one of the opportunities you identified in the previous activity? What will you change to better serve your customers, revolutionize your industry, and maintain your ultimate purpose?

_____

_____

_____

_____

_____

What resources, people, and organizational structure will best serve you as you go to war?

_____

_____

_____

_____

_____

_____

Imagine that you are 12 to 24 months in, and you are progressing toward your goals and winning the war. How do your resources, people, and organizational structure need to change? What will you need to support continued growth and progress?

_____

_____

_____

_____

_____

Some of your people may struggle to let go of their incremental attitude, so it will be important to take an active leadership role throughout the war. You need to be visible, consistent, and clear in your expectations. How will you communicate your organization's progress and help them stay motivated to push through the inevitable fog of war?

_____

_____

_____

_____

5

Put Execution Ahead of Strategy

Strategy and execution are equally important in business, but most people don't think deeply enough about execution, which is a mistake. It doesn't matter how great your strategy is if you can't execute it. And solid execution alone isn't enough for an organization to innovate and succeed. Organizations that can develop an excellent strategy and execute it well gain a competitive advantage over those that have great ideas but cannot effectively implement them. Once you've developed the right strategy to grow your business, execution is critically important as you scale.

The following activities will help you determine a strategy that is worth pursuing. They will also help you, your team, and your organization figure out how to execute and overcome challenges along the way.

SET A CAREER PATH FOR EXECUTION EXCELLENCE

Having a clear path to management roles can help your people learn by doing. Each career level will prepare them to take on more responsibility. As they learn how to better execute, they will also think more strategically. Consider the Snowflake sales levels, which support salespeople as they gain experience and are promoted to more senior roles (see the accompanying figure).

Establish a path for your managers to learn execution through experience. It should progress three or four levels to prepare your executive team to make decisions, develop department-level strategy, and execute. Summarize the roles, responsibilities, and outcomes for each level, keeping both strategy and execution in mind.

| Level 1 | Level 2 | Level 3 | Level 4 |

These people are your in-house consultants. They will develop a strategy that is more likely to work because they are also in operational roles. While the CEO also acts as the chief strategy officer, everyone in a management role is responsible for organizational strategy.

Now apply this career path to your own professional trajectory. Focus on what you will execute in each role. Where do you imagine your path will take you as you level up in your career?

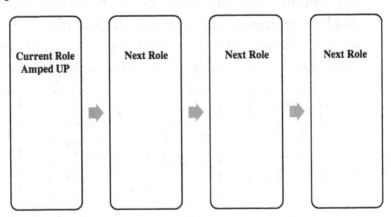

| Current Role Amped UP | Next Role | Next Role | Next Role |

EVALUATE YOUR EXECUTION: ON YOUR OWN

It can be easy to follow old decision-making patterns determining how to execute strategy. To minimize the impact of groupthink, complete this activity on your own, without discussing your responses with colleagues. Be honest in your answers. If you think of something that makes you feel uncomfortable, write it down and figure out why.

1. Summarize your current strategy:

   _____

   _____

   _____

   _____

2. Keep an open mind and turn a critical eye on how you are currently executing. If you were to fail in your execution, what would be the most likely reasons?

   _____

   _____

   _____

   _____

   _____

   _____

3. What steps can you take to prevent failure? How can you ensure your execution achieves your strategy?

   _____

   _____

   _____

   _____

   _____

   _____

4. Write a wish list of things that would help you successfully execute your strategy. Imagine there are no limits (e.g., budget, resources, time, culture, competing interests, etc.) and that you will be granted whatever you ask for.

_____

_____

_____

_____

_____

_____

5. How can you amp up your execution? What steps will you take to push yourself to the next level?

_____

_____

_____

_____

_____

_____

CONSIDER ALTERNATIVES

Discuss potential alternatives to your current strategy and execution. Don't discount any just because they are not the way you typically do things. Don't eliminate any options because they haven't worked in the past or at other organizations. Don't worry about squishy characteristics like fit, culture, or gut feeling.

Try to be optimistic about the number of options that are available to you and write down as many as you can, creating a numbered list in the table provided.

Execution Alternatives	Strategy Alternatives

Review your list of alternatives and identify the ones that you think could work best for your organization. Write down why you think each one would work well and what you would have to change to implement it effectively.

_____

_____

_____

_____

_____

_____

_____

_____

_____

_____

_____

_____

_____

_____

_____

_____

_____

_____

Which of these alternatives is most appealing? Why? Remember that changes to execution should come before any changes to your strategy.

With this in mind, how do you think your current execution stacks up? What changes would you make, if any? Would you consider replacing anything with one of the alternatives you identified? Why?

EVALUATE YOUR STRATEGY: WITH YOUR TEAM

After you've evaluated your strategy on your own, set aside time with your leadership team to share your responses, pinpoint weaknesses, and develop alternatives. Do not assume that differences in your answers are signs that someone is right and someone else is wrong. Those discrepancies can help you determine weak spots in your strategy—or opportunities you may have overlooked. During this conversation, encourage creative thinking. Every idea is worth considering, so keep an open mind.

1. Compare your summary with those prepared by your colleagues and discuss differences in your answers. Reflect on this conversation and what it reveals about your strategy and your organization's ability to execute it. As a group, revise your current strategy so everyone is in agreement. Write that unified strategy here.

   _____

   _____

   _____

   _____

2. Discuss the potential reasons why people believe you might fail in your execution. Write them down here.

   _____

   _____

   _____

   _____

   _____

   _____

   _____

   _____

3. As a group, discuss how you can prevent failure. What does this reveal about the effectiveness of your execution and the soundness of your strategy? Is your plan realistic? If not, where are the most likely problems with your strategy and execution?

   _____

   _____

   _____

_____

_____

_____

4. Discuss the wish lists. How can you eliminate execution
   problems? Remember that without strong execution, it's
   impossible to know whether your strategy is failing. You
   must fix your execution problems before assessing
   your strategy.

_____

_____

_____

_____

_____

5. Share answers about what people would change about the
   current strategy and/or execution? What weak points does
   this reveal? How should you consider changing your strategy or execution? Why?

_____

_____

_____

_____

_____

_____

6

Hire Drivers, Not Passengers, and Get the Wrong People Off the Bus

Once you have raised your standards, you need to objectively evaluate your people. You will be relying on them to execute the changes you are making, so they must be able to adopt an "Amp It Up" approach to their work. The people who are most prepared to do this are drivers. Passengers are the people who are satisfied being carried along but do little to contribute to the organization's momentum. Leaders need to do three things to effectively manage their workforce: get rid of passengers, place people in the right roles, and actively recruit drivers.

The following activities will help you identify passengers, cultivate drivers, and develop a plan to staff your organization over the long term.

DRIVERS AND PASSENGERS

Most people act like drivers some of the time and at other times like passengers. This can make it hard to put people into categories, even when evaluating ourselves. This activity can be useful to assess yourself and your team. To determine if you are more driver or passenger, consider the following statements and determine whether you are more likely to agree with response A or response B.

Statement	A	B
1. When facing a new and challenging project, I am most likely to:	Feel excited to get started and push through the difficult areas, even if I step on some toes along the way.	Look for potential pitfalls and adjust the process or goals to make it easier for everyone.
2. My style of goal setting could best be described by the following quote:	"Set realistic goals, keep reevaluating, and be consistent." —Attributed to Venus Williams (and others)	"A goal is not always meant to be reached. It often serves simply as something to aim at." —Attributed to Bruce Lee

(continued)

Statement	A	B
3. I usually defer to more senior colleagues because they have more experience and best understand how things work.	Mostly agree	Mostly disagree
4. If I could choose to hire a colleague for a similar position to mine, I would choose:	The applicant with a track record of making slow and reliable progress, without ever failing to meet their targets.	The applicant who has taken big risks, and has both some major failures and big successes in their work history.
5. Which of the following is more important to me in the workplace?	Confidence	Consensus
6. My dream job would be:	At a large, established organization, where I could expect a stable, long-term career.	At an underdog organization that is rethinking their strategy and business model.
7. I prefer a work environment that:	Allows me to fully invest myself in work that is unpredictable, where the stakes are high and I am pushed to my limits.	Is not overly demanding and where I know what to expect day to day and year to year.

Score your results using the following:

1. A = 1; B = 0
2. A = 0; B = 1
3. A = 0; B = 1
4. A = 0; B = 1
5. A = 1; B = 0
6. A = 0; B = 1
7. A = 1; B = 0

Your total _____

Driver/Passenger Score:

0–3: Passenger

4–7: Driver

With your results in mind, consider how you can develop your driver capabilities by answering the question that applies to you:

- If you have a driver score, what behaviors can you adopt to continue to contribute to your organization?
- If you have a passenger score, what specific actions and changes can you take to become a driver?

_____

_____

_____

_____

_____

_____

_____

Reflect on the answer to the previous question. Do you want to make these changes? Why or why not?

_____

_____

_____

_____

_____

What does this tell you about your career trajectory at this organization?

_____

_____

_____

_____

_____

_____

Ask your direct reports to score themselves without sharing their score. Meet with them individually to discuss where your organization is headed, and how they can work more aggressively to go after team and organizational goals. Inevitably, managers will already have a sense of who is a driver and who is a passenger. When meeting with suspected passengers, provide straightforward guidance and behaviors that will help them shift into the driver's seat.

MAKE ROOM FOR MORE DRIVERS

Removing people from their positions is not easy, but there are high costs to keeping the wrong people on the bus. First, they can undermine your progress by resisting change, compromising your standards, and sapping your organization's energy when you need it most. Second, every passenger comes with an opportunity cost. Every seat filled by a passenger represents a driver you cannot hire. To make space for the people you need, you have to jettison the people who are holding you back.

What does your ideal team look like? Describe what characteristics and behaviors are important and why.

_____

_____

_____

_____

_____

What is at stake if you fail to get the right people on the bus? What would the consequences be and who will bear them?

_____

_____

_____

_____

What is your reorganization plan for creating your ideal work-force? How will you decide who to replace or eliminate? What roles will you need to hire for immediately and what are their responsibilities?

_____

_____

_____

_____

_____

How will you communicate this to your team? Include key milestones for when you will make hard decisions.

_____

_____

_____

_____

_____

DRIVE ACTIVE RECRUITMENT

To support your organization's growth, you are going to need to be able to hire the right people quickly. There are two steps to active recruitment:

1. Plan for upcoming needs.
2. Maintain a list of potential candidates.

We'll look more closely at each of these steps in the following questions.

1. **Plan for upcoming needs.** Look at your long-term strategic plan. What roles will you need to fill in the next 3, 6, 12, and 24 months to support your growth?

   3 months:

   _____

   6 months:

   _____

   12 months:

   _____

   24 months:

   _____

2. **Maintain a list of potential candidates.** You can't grow quickly if it takes too long to vet candidates and fill positions. If someone is a valuable employee, you must have a plan to replace them if they leave for any reason. Create a list of potential candidates for each critical role you are responsible for, including why you think they would be optimal hires.

Role	Potential Candidate	Reasoning

Update this list whenever you have a performance discussion with people in these roles or as you review your upcoming staffing needs.

PERFORM ACTIVE CALIBRATION

Regular calibration sessions help you honestly and objectively evaluate your team. Your executives and managers should do this regularly, so determine the cadence that will work for you. The key is to use it to be proactive and catch issues early, so consider making this a regular quarterly activity. It could also occur as part of project debriefing.

Manager Evaluation

Before an active calibration session, executives and managers should evaluate their direct reports. The following questions should be considered alongside each department's targets and the organization's overall strategic goals. For each person, answer the following questions.

1. What are this person's strengths and most valuable qualities? What contributions have they made since the last calibration session?

   _____

   _____

   _____

   _____

2. What are this person's weaknesses? Where do they underperform? What makes them less than ideal as an employee?

   _____

   _____

   _____

   _____

3. What advice or training would you offer to this person? How will you know if it helped them improve their performance?

_____

_____

_____

_____

4. Do you consider this person to be a driver or a passenger? Why? Cite specific examples.

_____

_____

_____

_____

Peer Evaluation

Ask the same questions of peers of the evaluated employee who are outside the manager's chain of command. This will balance the manager's evaluation by bringing in other opinions.

1. What are this person's strengths and most valuable qualities? What contributions have they made since the last calibration session?

_____

_____

_____

2. What are this person's weaknesses? Where do they underperform? What makes them less than ideal as an employee?

_____

_____

_____

_____

3. What advice or training would you offer to this person? How will you know if it helped them improve their performance?

_____

_____

_____

_____

4. Do you consider this person to be a driver or a passenger? Why? Cite specific examples.

_____

_____

_____

_____

Calibration

After managers review the peer evaluation, they should answer the following questions.

Positive qualities: What positive qualities did the peer reviews reveal that you did not recognize? How can you leverage this opportunity to draw more on this person's strengths?

_____

_____

_____

_____

_____

_____

_____

Negative qualities: What negative qualities did the peer reviews reveal that you did not recognize? How can you address these performance gaps? How much time will you give the person to show improvement?

_____

_____

_____

_____

_____

_____

Driver or passenger: Do most people consider this person to be a driver or a passenger? How does this impact your evaluation of them and their work?

_____

_____

_____

_____

7

Build a Strong Culture

An organization's culture must serve its mission. The culture at a high-growth enterprise will be very different than the one in an organization that is satisfied with incremental progress or one in decline. While some companies prioritize making people feel happy at work, the resulting culture cannot support hypergrowth. The right culture is cohesive, consistent, and principled—and it can be a powerful driver of performance.

The following activities will help you develop a culture that aligns with your mission and growth trajectory. You will also come up with a plan to ensure the culture is consistently supported and how you will deal with behavior that threatens it.

CLARIFY YOUR CULTURAL VALUES

Culture can seem abstract, so it can be helpful to pinpoint your key values. At Data Domain, we used this R-E-C-I-P-E:

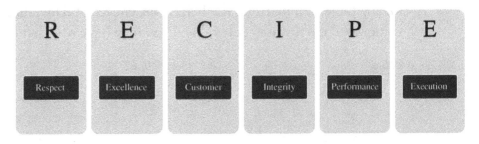

R	E	C	I	P	E
Respect	Excellence	Customer	Integrity	Performance	Execution

You are welcome to steal this, customize it, or create your own. To make sure your choice aligns with your mission, use the following space to brainstorm. What are your organization's key cultural values?

_____

_____

_____

_____

_____

Discuss your responses with your leadership team and select the ones that everyone can agree on. There is no strict rule about how many cultural values an organization has. I recommend picking between three and eight to keep things manageable. Write them down here:

_____   _____

_____   _____

_____   _____

_____   _____

It's fine to rely on this list, but if an acronym jumps out at you that people agree is a great fit, that's fine. Now it's time to examine what each of these values looks like in your organization. Complete the following table, summarizing the behaviors, effects, and meaning of each value. Use one row for each value. (You may have rows left over.)

Value	Description

CULTURE THROUGH ACCOUNTABILITY

In an organization with a strong culture, everyone is accountable for their actions. In places where the culture is consistent, people even call one another out for violating cultural values. But reaching that point is difficult. The only way to get there is by applying consequences consistently to reinforce desired behavior and to penalize anyone who acts against the cultural values.

How can you stay aware of outbreaks of bad culture? What policies and processes can you put in place to ensure your actual culture aligns with your stated values?

_____

_____

_____

_____

_____

_____

How can you create an environment where people feel comfortable reporting behavior that violates your cultural values? What systems have been put in place, or need to be put in place? How are you protecting (or how will you protect) people who make legitimate complaints?

_____

_____

_____

_____

_____

_____

What steps can you take now to make it easier to part with people who undermine your culture and violate your organization's values? How will you deal with a high performer who disregards your standards?

_____

_____

_____

_____

_____

PROTECT YOUR CULTURE

What is your plan to evaluate your culture as it takes root? How will you check in with frontline employees to ensure your values are being consistently applied?

_____

_____

_____

_____

_____

What changes can you make to your hiring and onboarding process to ensure new employees take your values seriously?

_____

_____

_____

_____

_____

How can you stay aligned with your leadership team to ensure you are all applying these principles consistently? How can you ensure you are all holding your teams accountable?

_____

_____

_____

_____

_____

_____

8

Teach Everyone to Go Direct and Build Mutual Trust

Two major challenges in aligning people and culture are silos and lack of trust. Leaders should build on their organization's mission and cultural values to encourage employees to work across departments. When everyone is working toward the same mission and top-level strategy, it's easier to tear down silos. A more unified, cross-functional workforce sets the foundation for increasing trust among colleagues. When your organizational culture supports trust, respect, and integrity, people will feel more comfortable speaking up and making decisions. They will also act with a greater sense of commitment and accountability.

The following activities will help you determine whether silos are a problem in your organization. They will also help you learn how to build trust and use it to perform at a higher level. Because these topics are so integral to teamwork, these activities will include a number of sections for your team to complete.

IDENTIFY SILOS

To fully realize your strategy and mission, different functions must work together. Even when people execute well within their departmental silos, performance is limited until teams can work together across different functional units. To determine if silos are a problem in your organization, ask your team to answer the following questions anonymously. Complete them yourself as well.

1. Aside from your manager, with whom do you work most closely in the course of your daily work and on special projects? Include the person's name and department, and mention a success you created together.

Name	Department	Shared Success

2. What roles from other departments do you work with on a daily basis?

_____

_____

_____

3. What roles from other departments do you work with on a weekly basis?

_____

_____

_____

4. How often do you collaborate with colleagues from other departments?
   a. Daily
   b. Several times a week
   c. Several times a month
   d. Less frequently than several times a month

5. How are you most likely to initially address issues with peers in other departments?
   a. I contact them directly to discuss the issue and we resolve it on our own.
   b. I contact them directly and copy one or both of our managers to document the issue and how we resolved it.
   c. I contact my manager or theirs to resolve the issue for me.
   d. I ask for a meeting with them and one or both of our managers to discuss the issue and resolve it together.

6. How are you most likely to initially address issues with someone who outranks you in another department?
   a. I contact them directly to discuss the issue and we resolve it on our own.
   b. I contact them directly and copy one or both of our managers to document the issue and how we resolved it.
   c. I ask my manager or theirs to resolve the issue for me.
   d. I ask for a meeting with them and one or both of our managers to discuss the issue and resolve it together.

7. How are you most likely to initially address issues with someone you outrank in another department?

   a. I contact them directly to discuss the issue and we resolve it on our own.

   b. I contact them directly and copy one or both of our managers to document the issue and how we resolved it.

   c. I ask my manager or theirs to resolve the issue for me.

   d. I ask for a meeting with them and one or both of our managers to discuss the issue and resolve it together.

8. If you don't contact a colleague directly, what are the reasons?

_____

_____

_____

GO DIRECT

After you and your team have completed the activity "Identify Silos," reflect on what you as a leader can do to demolish them and encourage people to go direct.

Review your team's responses from the "Identify Silos" activity. What do they tell you about silos in your organization? *Are particular teams or departments more siloed than others? Are certain people or teams more approachable than others?*

_____

_____

_____

_____

_____

Consider how you would feel if you found out one of your direct reports contacted someone of a higher rank in another department directly to ask a question. How would you react once you found out? *Your response will help determine if you contribute to silos.*

If you want to demolish silos, you must be able to explain to your team what types of issues you need to be involved in and what types of things you expect them to resolve directly. You should encourage your team to go direct as often as possible, but it can be reassuring to you and them to understand what kinds of issues require a larger discussion.

Go direct for the following types of issues, questions, and problems:

Bring in a manager for the following types of issues, questions, and problems:

You can use this to encourage your team to go direct, regardless of their role, while also ensuring that serious issues get the attention they deserve.

STEP INTO A HIGH-TRUST ENVIRONMENT

A high-trust environment requires people to be upfront about their mistakes. While this can be difficult to acknowledge, it's important that you be open about your role in things when they don't go well. This will help your team understand that they can also admit their mistakes to fully address a situation.

Describe the last time you made a mistake that affected your team or your organization. What was the error and how did you address it?

_____

_____

_____

_____

_____

How did you admit your mistake to your team or your colleagues? If you did not publicly admit your error, why not? What did you do instead?

_____

_____

_____

_____

What were the effects of that decision? What message did your admission, or lack thereof, send to the people you work with?

_____

_____

_____

The next time you make an error, what steps will you take to hold yourself publicly accountable? Why?

_____

_____

_____

_____

9

Put Analysis Before Solutions

The business world tends to be so motivated to implement solutions that they often begin making major changes before fully analyzing the problems they are trying to solve. In some cases, especially at large, established companies, leaders begin looking to make changes while ignoring the reasons, risks, and implications of their decisions. Groupthink and bias are often behind these tendencies, but by making the conscious choice to focus on analysis, most people can break these patterns and improve their decisions.

The following activities will help you identify the root causes of problems by showing you how to use first principles thinking to analyze decisions about your business. Remember that first principles thinking is a way of breaking problems down into their foundational elements and removing assumptions.

WHEN THE SOLUTION IS THE PROBLEM

Start by thinking of a business problem that you failed to properly analyze before moving ahead with a solution. When did you realize that you had made the wrong decision? What were the implications of that decision?

_____

_____

_____

_____

_____

_____

_____

_____

Had you thoroughly analyzed the situation, what would you have noticed? What were the signs that you were on the wrong track?

_____

_____

_____

_____

_____

DIAGNOSE YOUR PROBLEM

Leaders should act more like doctors and focus on analyzing a problem before prescribing a remedy. It takes practice to develop this skill, so you may want to do this activity more than once.

Consider a problem, challenge, or opportunity that your organization is currently facing. What are the symptoms that something is wrong? What is the reason you need to change? *Your answer here will likely be based on performance issues, metrics, or some other data that may seem clear-cut.*

_____

_____

_____

_____

To look past the symptoms to the root causes, you need to engage in careful analysis and imagine that you have never seen this problem before. Don't lean on assumptions. Consider every possible angle. Instead of looking at the entire problem as a whole, break it down into parts.

What are all the factors that could be contributing to this problem? *If you get stuck, ask yourself, "What if it's not any of these?" Consider the perspectives of different departments and people at different levels of the organization. What might they suggest?*

_____

_____

_____

_____

_____

_____

_____

_____

It's time to get a second opinion. Seek counsel from a few people outside of your immediate team, department, or organization. Describe the symptoms you are facing, and ask them to analyze the problem and come up with potential reasons why it is happening. What did they consider that you did not?

_____

_____

_____

_____

Apply first principles thinking to the problem and your lists. First principles are the fundamental parts of the problem that do not stem from anything else. This approach can help you determine the root causes.

Which of the issues on your previous lists cannot be deduced any further? Which issues do not stem from other parts of the problem?

_____

_____

_____

_____

You can repeat this activity to dig deeper into the problem at the department level, or you can use this approach to analyze another problem or potential opportunity. You will get better at thinking in this way with more practice.

PRE-INTERVIEW PLANNING

When a key role must be filled, it can be tempting to hire someone who seems good enough and convince yourself you can train them to be a better fit. In reality, it makes more sense to hire the right person from the start. Fine-tuning your interview process can help you make sure that you are making the best hiring decision.

What questions can you ask to be certain you make a complete and accurate analysis of this candidate?

_____

_____

_____

_____

_____

_____

_____

_____

_____

_____

_____

_____

Once you have your list of questions, decide who will be part of the interview. Include peer-level employees, who will be able to assess the applicant from a different perspective. Complete the following evaluations.

Evaluation

During and after an interview, hiring managers and the new hire's potential peers should evaluate applicants. Consider each person's performance alongside the job position and the organization's overall strategic goals. For each applicant, answer the following questions.

1. What are this candidate's strengths and most valuable qualities for the position?

   _____

   _____

   _____

   _____

2. What are this person's weaknesses? What might they struggle with most in this position?

   _____

   _____

   _____

   _____

NEW-HIRE CALIBRATION

The first 30 to 90 days should give you a good picture of a new hire's performance and potential. The new hire's first active calibration will reveal a lot about whether they are the right person for the job. Consider the following questions as you conduct the person's first active calibration.

Positive qualities: What strengths has this person demonstrated in their new role? What positive qualities did the peer reviews reveal that you did not recognize? How can you leverage these opportunities to draw more on this person's strengths?

_____

_____

_____

_____

_____

_____

Negative qualities: What negative qualities did your evaluation and the peer reviews indicate? Can you address these performance gaps? How will you assess the new hire to ensure they are executing as needed? How much time will they have to improve their performance?

_____

_____

_____

_____

_____

_____

Driver or passenger: Do most people consider this person to be a driver or a passenger? How does this impact your evaluation of them and their potential to contribute to your organization?

_____

_____

_____

IMPROVING FUTURE ANALYSIS

Consider your new hire's first active calibration. What questions could you include in future interviews with applicants to get a better sense of the strengths and weaknesses as they emerge in this position?

_____

_____

_____

_____

_____

_____

_____

10

Align Incentives for Customer Success

Customer success is the business of the entire organization. Dedicated "customer success" departments can undermine an organization's mission and sense of cohesion. If your teams are organized appropriately and held accountable for their goals, customer success should happen naturally. To resolve customer problems and grievances, a better approach is to make sure each team feels ownership for their role in resolving customer issues and ensuring client satisfaction. Keeping customer success integrated also reduces complexity, making it easier to solve problems and maintain client relationships.

The following activity will help you establish ownership over client relationships and success.

SUPPORT YOUR CUSTOMERS AT EVERY LEVEL

Everyone has a role in your clients' success. Your job is to incentivize your people to feel connected to how your customers are doing. Complete the following table to specify what each departmental function is responsible for in ensuring customer success.

Department	Role in the Client Experience

If your organization has a dedicated customer success team, consider whether it would be better for all your people to be invested in your customers' success. How could returning the client success roles to the relevant departments change day-to-day work at your organization?

_____

_____

_____

_____

_____

Consider your mission statement (Chapter 3) and cultural values (Chapter 7). How can you better serve those key elements by integrating your customer success throughout your organization?

_____

_____

_____

_____

_____

11

Ramp Up Sales

It can be hard to tell when an organization is ready to ramp up sales and focus on hypergrowth. Until you reach that point, it makes sense to have a sales person who can take on more of a business development role, pinpointing one excellent opportunity at a time. Once your product or service is ready to scale (and not before then), you'll need to have a sales force in place. As you build this team, pay close attention to each individual's progress or lack of progress. If they are not succeeding, what can you do to fix that?

The following activities will help you determine what kind of sales team you need and how to improve their efficiency.

GET THE TIMING RIGHT

It's a mistake to ramp up your sales too early, but if you wait too long, you'll miss key growth opportunities. As you try to determine when the time is right, consider the following questions.

1. Are you happy with your current sales productivity metrics? If not, how can you improve productivity before adding more sales headcount?

   _____

   _____

   _____

2. Are you happy with the metrics of your lead generation pipeline? If not, how can you improve it?

   _____

   _____

   _____

3. Are you being realistic in your timeline of sales targets? Are you projecting too much too soon, or too little too late?

_____

_____

_____

4. Are you being aggressive enough and thinking big enough to outpace your competition? If not, how will you change your sales approach to better align with your strategic goals?

_____

_____

_____

5. Is your sales team buying into your targets and timeline? Are they owning the goals and fully committed to hitting them? If not, what are their concerns or blockers?

_____

_____

_____

6. Reflect on your responses. What can you conclude about whether your organization is ready for you to ramp up sales? If you're not ready now, when will you know the time is right?

_____

_____

_____

CROSS THE CHASM

Consider how sales will help you execute your overall strategy. How will you know when to conserve resources and when to scale? How will your metrics let you know it's time to pivot?

_____

_____

_____

_____

Imagine you are ready to cross the chasm and begin selling to the mass market. How will you approach each of the following sales functions to support growth as you scale?

1. **Lead Generation:** How will you ensure your salespeople have enough leads to pursue? What kind of pipeline coverage will you need?

   _____

   _____

   _____

2. **Closing:** How will you add sales reps over the next 12 to 18 months? What qualities will you look for?

   _____

   _____

   _____

3. **Servicing the Sale:** How will you expect your sales reps to be involved in customer service? How will you protect your sales reps' time while also ensuring your customers are taken care of?

   _____

   _____

   _____

ESTABLISH YOUR PROCESS

In order to succeed, you must have a trainable, scalable sales process that every sales rep can execute and repeat. Consider what your gunslingers (your most effective salespeople) do, and use that information to define a process. Answer the following questions to outline your sales process.

1. How much prospecting should your sales team do each day or week? How will you determine whether a pipeline has enough leads?

   _____

   _____

2. What conditions must be met in order to qualify a lead as a true prospect?

   _____

   _____

3. How should sales reps reach out to prospects? What steps should they take to establish and maintain those relationships?

   _____

   _____

4. What should sales reps cover in the first meeting? If there is a second meeting, how should your sales reps prepare for that?

   _____

   _____

5. What signs or actions indicate that it is time to attempt to close the sale? What closing techniques should your sales reps use?

_____

_____

6. How and when should sales reps consider upselling or cross-selling?

_____

_____

7. Consider the steps in your process. Draw a picture of your sales process or funnel to clarify how the steps unfold. Include dates for how much time you expect each step to take:

_____

_____

_____

_____

_____

_____

EVALUATING RESOURCES

To ensure your sales team can be efficient and deliver the growth you need, consider how you will evaluate them and provide the support they need to thrive.

1. How will you set quotas for your salespeople? What metrics will you use and how will you apply this data to individuals?

_____

_____

_____

_____

_____

2. If an individual fails to reach their quota, what kinds of training or resources will you provide? How will you help them improve before their next evaluation?

_____

_____

_____

_____

3. If your sales team overall is struggling, what questions will you ask to determine the reasons?

_____

_____

_____

_____

4. How will you know when to add or cut headcount among your sales force? What data will you use to make these decisions?

_____

_____

_____

_____

5. What will you expect your managers to provide to best support your sales team as they grow your sales?

_____

_____

_____

12

Grow Fast or Die Slow

It's not unusual for leaders to pump the brakes because they are uncertain or fearful that they won't be able to effectively manage as their company grows. Having a growth model in place can help organizations determine whether their business will scale successfully or whether it will struggle to reach profitability. Planning in advance also helps you prepare to move into adjacent markets or innovate within a core product rather than trying to innovate a second or third product from scratch. Growing is hard as a startup, but it can become even more difficult once you've reached scale.

The following activities will help you understand what to expect and how to approach hypergrowth, beat the competition, and continue to grow long term.

BUILD YOUR GROWTH MODEL

Trying to scale without a plan in place is like trying to build a house without a blueprint. It can be difficult to determine the limits and potential of scale, and a growth model can help you get clarity.

Consider the realities of your business landscape as you answer the following questions. To ensure you are considering all angles, have your team answer these questions as well. You'll compare your responses at the end of this activity.

1. What factors can support or limit your organization's growth? List all key considerations or elements that relate to your market, the business landscape, your product, and so on.

   _____

   _____

   _____

   _____

   _____

_____

_____

2. What is the biggest factor that could limit your organization's growth? What is your biggest concern? Describe a few ways you could address it.

_____

_____

_____

_____

_____

_____

3. What is an ambitious growth target for your organization? What steps will your organization or your leadership team take to reach for that growth target?

_____

_____

_____

_____

_____

Discuss your responses with your team, noting new ideas.

1. What compelling factors were not on your list? What can this tell you about potential blind spots?

_____

_____

_____

_____

_____

_____

_____

2. As a group, decide what the two biggest limitations are to your organization's growth. What would be the best way to address these and minimize their impact? What teams or people should be put in place and what should they do?

_____

_____

_____

_____

_____

3. As a group, decide what two factors will be most helpful to you as you grow. How can you best harness them to maximize their impact? What teams or people should be put in place and what should they do?

_____

_____

_____

_____

_____

4. Consider your previous responses and envision your company's growth trajectory. As you scale, how will expenses and compensation plans need to shift in relation to revenue? Provide specific metrics and details by department and function.

_____

_____

_____

_____

_____

_____

_____

5. Using the information you've discussed, describe your organization's growth model here.

_____

_____

_____

_____

_____

_____

_____

BEATING THE COMPETITION

Hypergrowth can distinguish you from the competition, but to use this as an edge, you must plan. List your top competitors and describe their business models.

Competitor	Business Model

How does your growth model set your organization apart?

_____

_____

_____

_____

_____

What actions can you take to dominate the market and steal business from your competitors while generating net new revenue?

_____

_____

_____

_____

_____

_____

KEEP GETTING BIGGER

Look into a perfect distant future where your organization has successfully pursued its growth model and gotten big. Consider how you can continue to grow. Your new business model will be determined by the untapped growth potential in your market and in your product lines.

What are key traits, needs, wants, and characteristics of your primary market? What are you looking for in new markets as you expand?

_____

_____

_____

Does your organization have the ability to develop and bring to market another truly innovative product? If so, what is it and how would it be different than anything that already exists?

_____

_____

_____

Identify three adjacent markets that could offer untapped demand. Consider the needs of each one and research how you think you could meet them. What changes would you need to make?

Adjacent Market	Meeting Market Needs

MANAGING COSTS

Your organization's cost structure needs to optimize for higher growth rates and bigger goals. That means applying resources aggressively, while fixing misallocated resources. What departments or organizations will need to reduce costs as you scale? Why?

_____

_____

_____

_____

_____

How can you change compensation plans at the department level to ensure they incentivize the right behavior and balance your costs?

_____

_____

_____

_____

_____

How can you change contracts or agreements with clients to prioritize revenue and ensure your organization can sustain itself long term? Who do you need to work with internally to formalize and roll out these changes?

_____

_____

_____

_____

_____

_____

_____

_____

_____

_____

13

Stay Scrappy as You Scale Up

The paradox of scaling up is that, as companies do so, they tend to outgrow their scrappiness and lose their dynamism. However, that is a recipe for failure, no matter how well you penetrate the market. Your company's stage of development determines your approach to resourcing and leading your team. You cannot run a 10-person team the same way you run a 500-person organization, so understanding what your organization needs to work through each stage of development is critical—as is having a leader who can adapt to the company's shifting approach.

The following activities will help determine the most appropriate, efficient, and affordable way of doing business.

PEG YOUR EXPENSES TO YOUR STAGE OF DEVELOPMENT

There are three main phases of a company's development, and each one demands different types of leadership:

1. Embryonic: The smallest stage of a startup, when the team is small and close-knit.
2. Formative: When there is enough product to begin testing the market.
3. Scaled-up: When the company serves a large market after rapid adoption.

Consider your company's characteristics, personnel, and relationship with your market. What stage do you think you are in? Why? Describe the greatest challenges you are facing regarding your organization's growth.

_____

_____

_____

_____

_____

_____

_____

   Consider whether your spending efficiency and operating efficiency are appropriate for your organization's development level.
What changes could you make to your operations, cash flow, and
expenses to help your company successfully cross the chasm
and scale?

_____

_____

_____

_____

_____

_____

   If you are in the embryonic or formative stage of development,
how will you know when you've crossed the chasm and become a
scaled-up company? What changes will you need to make to support this shift?

_____

_____

_____

_____

_____

_____

THE RIGHT LEADER FOR YOUR STATE OF DEVELOPMENT

Your purpose as a leader is to determine the best way to scale up your company while holding on to early-stage dynamism. To keep a clear mind in the face of change, it's important to recognize how your past experience influences you, and to plan for the big changes that are coming.

How has your leadership changed as your organization has grown?

_____

_____

_____

_____

_____

_____

_____

If your organization could do just one thing for the remainder of the year, what would it be and why?

_____

_____

_____

_____

_____

_____

Reflect on your mission statement (Chapter 3) and growth model (Chapter 12), then discuss the following questions with your team.

What are we not currently doing that we urgently need to do?

_____

_____

_____

_____

_____

_____

What is something we are doing now that has only a marginal impact but consumes valuable time and resources?

_____

_____

_____

_____

_____

_____

Based on your answers above, what changes will you pursue? How will you measure their impact?

_____

_____

_____

_____

_____

_____

How will you help your organization stay scrappy as you scale? How will you know your efforts are paying off?

_____

_____

_____

_____

_____

_____

_____

14

Materialize Your Opportunities

Revisiting your organization's growth story can help you get a handle on the opportunities you're facing. If you're not consciously looking for ways to grow, you'll miss out. Apply the nine takeaways from Data Domain's growth story to fine-tune your strategy and map your course.

The following activities will help you hone your strategy and build the story of your organization's future growth. Before you begin, revisit your strategy from Chapter 5 and summarize it here.

_____

_____

_____

_____

SURVEY THE LANDSCAPE

Takeaways 1 and 2 concern the industry conditions on the ground. Consider the popular incumbents and up-and-coming competitors in your space.

Takeaway 1: Attack weakness, not strength.

What do your customers and potential customers hate about their current vendor? What do they want to change? What do your competitors do poorly?

_____

_____

_____

_____

_____

_____

_____

_____

Takeaway 2: Either create a cost advantage or neutralize someone else's.

How can you best use economic factors to your advantage? If you can't beat a competitor on price, what can you offer to present a better value?

_____

_____

_____

_____

_____

_____

TAKE THE MARKET'S VITALS

Takeaways 3–5 are about your market, which will change over time. Consider your current customers and your future ones.

Takeaway 3: It's much easier to attack an existing market than create a new one.

What market will you take over? How can you appeal to potential customers? How can you displace your competitors?

_____

_____

_____

_____

_____

_____

_____

_____

_____

_____

_____

Takeaway 4: Early adopters buy differently than later adopters.

Who are your early adopters and later adopters? What changes will you need to make to support later adopters and grow your market share?

_____

_____

_____

_____

_____

_____

_____

_____

Takeaway 5: Stay close to home in the early going.

Where are you likely to find prospective clients who share your ideals? That is where you need to be. What is your service plan once you get there? How will you keep your initial core of customers happy?

_____

_____

_____

_____

_____

_____

_____

_____

LOOK END TO END

Takeaway 6 encompasses a lot of ground because it encourages you to figure out how to offer a complete solution.

Takeaway 6: Build the whole product or solve the whole problem as fast as you can.

Consider the ideal customer experience, end to end. Where are the gaps in what you offer? How can you expand your solution so you can control and improve the entire customer experience?

_____

_____

_____

_____

_____

_____

DETERMINE YOUR TECH

Takeaways 7 and 8 deal with the more technical aspects of your product.

Takeaway 7: Bet on the correct enabling technologies.

What makes up your core technology? Who out there needs it most? How will it help you deliver a better product?

_____

_____

_____

_____

_____

_____

_____

Takeaway 8: Architecture is everything.

What is the ideal architecture for your product? If you don't offer a tech product, what sets your offering apart? How can you improve on what is currently offered?

_____

_____

_____

_____

_____

KEEP LOOKING AHEAD

Takeaway 9: Prepare to transform your strategy sooner than you expect.

What's your next move? How will you build on your core business?

_____

_____

_____

_____

_____

_____

_____

15

Open the Aperture

A strategy transformation takes planning and conscious effort. When determining whether an organization has the potential to be a super-grower, consider what their current customers think about the product and the people. Explore how you can improve the existing strategy before moving to transform it. Then look to expand opportunities that will help you outlast the competition.

The following activities will help you build on your existing strategy so you can expand your vision and your company.

IDENTIFY SUPER-GROWER POTENTIAL

Super-growers share four key factors:

1. Exceptional growth rate to date
2. Weak and unpopular incumbents in the market
3. Organic expansion with customers
4. Customer satisfaction and praise

Consider each of these in the context of your organization to determine your growth potential.

1. **Growth rate to date:** How quickly has your organization been growing? What does this tell you about its capacity for rapid expansion?

   _____

   _____

   _____

   _____

2. **Weak and unpopular incumbents in the market:** What is the competition like? Will they be hard to displace? In what ways are they vulnerable? What kind of relationships do they have with their clients?

_____

_____

_____

_____

3. **Organic customer expansion:** Are your customers finding new uses for your products? What does this tell you about how you can expand? What does this tell you about your product?

_____

_____

_____

_____

4. **Customer satisfaction and praise:** What is the overall tone of the feedback you receive? What does this tell you about how easy it will be for you to expand? Are you in danger of being displaced by an upstart? Or are you the better option customers have been waiting for? If not, how can you become the better option?

_____

_____

_____

_____

Based on your responses to these four questions, what do you think your super-grower potential is?

_____

_____

LAY THE GROUNDWORK FOR YOUR EXPANSION

Before you transform your strategy, make sure you've maximized your original one. Consider what you can do better and how you can grow within the targets you've set.

What untapped potential do you see in your original strategy? How can you improve execution to capture this?

_____

_____

_____

_____

_____

Now connect your original strategy with your future plans. How can capturing current untapped potential support your future growth? What is the connection between your current customers and your future customers?

_____

_____

_____

_____

_____

_____

What is the natural progression of your strategy transformation? Based on your existing strategy and execution, where are you headed?

_____

_____

_____

_____

_____

Does this align with your vision? If not, what needs to change? Why?

_____

_____

_____

_____

_____

_____

PLAN TO TRANSFORM YOUR STRATEGY

It's impossible to transform your strategy overnight. Consider what changes you must make to your product for it to fully realize your future strategy.

What will you change about your product? What will you need to add to your product line to fulfill your future strategy?

_____

_____

_____

_____

_____

_____

_____

It's not possible to do all of these things at once. In what order will you implement these changes? Why does this order make the most sense?

_____

_____

_____

_____

_____

_____

_____

_____

_____

_____

_____

_____

_____

_____

WIDEN THE APERTURE

To keep growing, you need to tap into new markets. What new markets can you reach as your strategy expands? Include the changes you'll need to make to connect with customers in these new markets.

_____

_____

_____

_____

_____

_____

_____

_____

How will you communicate your new strategy to existing customers and prospective clients?

_____

_____

_____

_____

_____

_____

_____

_____

ICE OUT THE COMPETITION

Consider your strategic path and the new markets you plan to enter. Who are the most threatening competitors you'll encounter? What are their competitive strengths?

_____

_____

_____

_____

_____

_____

_____

_____

How will you respond to this competitive edge? What changes can you make on a strategic level to build a moat of safety around your organization and your products?

_____

_____

_____

_____

_____

_____

_____

How will you execute these changes?

_____

_____

_____

_____

_____

_____

_____

16

Swing for the Fences

Strategic transformation requires lead time and foresight. You need to think well ahead of the current dynamic in your market to succeed, even if your strategy and product are exactly what the market wants and needs. To stay ahead of market shifts, management must understand how to reposition themselves for growth. You may think you have enough time to prepare for the future, but you probably don't. Anything essential to your strategy must be in place before anyone needs it. Don't take comfort in the status quo. Try to anticipate what's coming next.

The following activities will help you reposition your company as your strategy evolves.

PLAN THE NEXT SHIFT

Where do you think the market is going? How will the world in which you do business change as your strategy transforms?

_____

_____

_____

_____

_____

_____

Think about your current positioning. How could it pigeon-hole you or hold you back as the market's needs change?

_____

_____

_____

_____

_____

_____
_____
_____

How can you most effectively communicate each essential change to your strategy and positioning? What will you change in terms of your messaging, branding, and communications?

_____
_____
_____
_____
_____
_____
_____
_____

DEFINE YOUR STRATEGY EVOLUTION

Consider your responses to the questions in Chapters 14 through 16 against your current strategy.

Write your current strategy here.

_____
_____

How has your strategy shifted as you've improved your execution?

_____
_____
_____

Write your next strategy here.

_____

_____

_____

How will you get there? What will you need to execute?

_____

_____

_____

_____

Now try to see the future. Where do you think you'll go next?

_____

_____

_____

_____

What will be the biggest challenges to executing this strategy? How will you overcome them?

_____

_____

_____

_____

How can you futureproof your organization and pursue this strategy so you're already there even before you need to be?

_____

_____

_____

_____

_____

17

Amp Up Your Career

Like growing a company, developing your career can be an exciting challenge. The key is to focus on your experience and manage yourself like a product. Keep your long-term goals in mind and let them direct your path. Approach each role as an opportunity to build a record of accomplishments. This proves that you are a driver who is focused on outcomes—someone who can execute. Your aptitude, attitude, and behavior matter more than anything else when it comes to your career. Take time to understand your talents, and recognize your strengths and weaknesses—and adjust accordingly.

The following activities will help you pinpoint your goals, play up your strengths, and hone your self-awareness.

PRODUCT-MANAGE YOURSELF

Consider your career path to this point.

Are you satisfied with your upward progress to this point in your career? Why or why not?

_____

_____

_____

_____

What accomplishments are you particularly proud of? How would you describe them to someone who is interviewing you for a job?

_____

_____

_____

_____

_____

_____

_____

_____

_____

_____

_____

_____

Have you ever experienced a major setback? If so, what did you learn from it? What steps can you take to draw on that experience as you face future challenges?

_____

_____

_____

_____

_____

_____

_____

FIND YOUR APTITUDE

Consider your natural talents and abilities. What are you innately good at? Back up your claim with examples and stories that interviewers would find compelling.

_____

_____

_____

_____

_____

_____

_____

Tap into your self-awareness and consider your weaknesses. Be honest with yourself. What are your limitations? How can you adjust your work to better manage them?

_____

_____

_____

_____

_____

_____

_____

How would colleagues describe your personality?

_____

_____

_____

What aspects of your personality are most helpful in your career?

_____

_____

_____

What techniques can you use to keep your energy and optimism high, even during challenging professional moments?

_____

_____

_____

_____

_____

DEFINE YOUR PATH

What is your personal definition of career success? Imagine you are about to retire from your ideal career. What did you accomplish? What positions did you hold?

_____

_____

_____

_____

_____

What roles and projects have you enjoyed most? How have they drawn on your natural aptitude and personality?

_____

_____

_____

_____

_____

How do the roles and projects you identified above align with your personal definition of career success? Do you think you should make any changes to your definition of success in light of your natural abilities and personality?

_____

_____

_____

_____

STAY THE COURSE

Revisit the following questions quarterly with yourself. Discuss your findings with your manager to ensure your organization understands how you plan to develop professionally.

What path do you see for career advancement? How are you preparing for the next step or promotion?

_____

_____

_____

_____

What challenges do you struggle with? How are you working to improve your performance and fill any skill or knowledge gaps?

_____

_____

_____

_____

Do you believe you are able to pursue your professional goals at your current organization? If not, will you look elsewhere or seek out another role where you are that allows you to grow?

_____

_____

_____

_____

18

Not Just for CEOs: Dealing with Founders and Boards

Whether you're a CEO, you aspire to be one, or you don't see yourself in that role, you can still develop ways to think like an effective leader. Non-founder CEOs often want and need to change an organization's culture to realize their mission and goals. At the department level, new managers can run into similar challenges when they want to establish new ways of doing things. This can generate resistance among employees, so it's best to tread lightly at first and be respectful of your predecessor. As a leader, you will also need to manage your relationship with your board of directors, whether they are a formal part of your organization's structure or your personal board of advisors.

The following activities will help you navigate your relationships with the people who came before you and board.

UNPACK THE FOUNDER MYTHOLOGY

Begin by clarifying your vision for the next stage of your company or department. What is your role? What are the biggest untapped opportunities? What will be the biggest challenges?

_____

_____

_____

_____

_____

_____

_____

Do some research into your organization's founder or your predecessor. What is the true or not-so-true mythology surrounding their success? What is their role in the story of the company? What did people value about them?

_____

_____

_____

_____

_____

_____

What is the more realistic version of your founder or predecessor's story? Include any weaknesses or limitations that you have identified.

_____

_____

_____

_____

_____

_____

_____

_____

_____

How has this mythology affected your organization's culture? What changes to the culture will you need to make to improve performance?

_____

_____

_____

_____

_____

_____

_____

_____

TREAD LIGHTLY

Build on your responses from the previous activity. To avoid alienating employees, consider how you can change the culture in a three stage-process, as shown in the image seen here.

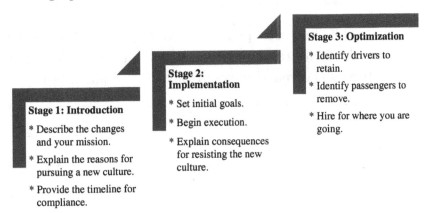

Stage 1: Introduction

* Describe the changes and your mission.

* Explain the reasons for pursuing a new culture.

* Provide the timeline for compliance.

Stage 2: Implementation

* Set initial goals.

* Begin execution.

* Explain consequences for resisting the new culture.

Stage 3: Optimization

* Identify drivers to retain.

* Identify passengers to remove.

* Hire for where you are going.

As a leader, you must start with Stage 1. Stages 2 and 3 are covered in other chapters, so we will focus on Stage 1 here.

Outline what you will communicate to your employees in Stage 1. What opportunities do you plan to pursue? Why do you need to change to make this shift?

_____

_____

_____

_____

_____

_____

_____

_____

How do the changes you describe build on your predecessor's vision?

_____

_____

_____

_____

Discuss your plan with your predecessor, or someone who worked with them closely, and ask for their feedback. Is there anything you can add to your Stage 1 communication?

_____

_____

_____

_____

What success story will you, the founder (or your predecessor), and your employees be telling after you execute this big change? Focus on how everyone will benefit.

_____

_____

_____

_____

_____

_____

_____

DEFINE THE BOARD'S ROLE

While the role of the board tends to blur with that of executive leadership, it can be helpful to establish early on the ideal relationship between the two.

Consider how you work best. What level of confidence and experience do you have as you enter your leadership role? How will you prepare yourself to reject advice that conflicts with your goals and values, or doesn't support your plan? If you are a CEO, how will you prepare to push back if the board seems unwilling to give you the authority you need to execute your strategy?

_____

_____

_____

_____

_____

_____

_____

_____

_____

Imagine how you would describe to the board the type of relationship that will work best for you. What is the ideal division of authority for you as a leader? What is the best way to balance the board's feedback with your autonomy?

_____

_____

_____

_____

_____

_____

_____

_____

_____

Discuss your responses with your board. Based on their reaction, what will be the biggest challenges you face when maintaining your autonomy?

_____

_____

_____

_____

How can you overcome those challenges?

_____

_____

_____

_____

LEAD YOUR BOARD

Before you approach your board, prepare to lead them by answering the following questions about the issues you plan to discuss.

What do you think you should do about this issue?

_____

_____

_____

_____

_____

How do you plan to execute your approach?

_____

_____

_____

_____

_____

How does your execution plan support the organization's strategy?

_____

_____

_____

_____

_____

What alternatives do you think your board members will propose?

_____

_____

_____

_____

_____

Why is your plan better?

_____

_____

_____

_____

_____

What questions do you think the board will have? List them and your answers here.

_____

_____

_____

_____

_____

CONSIDER YOUR PERSONAL BOARD

To be transparent, I don't rely on using other people as a sounding board because I prefer to follow my own methods and insights when it comes to amping things up. However, I can see how having a board's advice could be beneficial, especially for leaders who are relatively inexperienced. For example, when I reflect on Data Domain's acquisition, I know that I would have done things differently back then if I had the experience or insights I have today. At the time, I didn't know my own blind spots and that led me to an outcome that I consider to be less than ideal. Perhaps that is an argument in favor of cultivating a personal board of advisors.

To get the most value out of your personal board, you first must pinpoint your own weaknesses. What are your blind spots? Where do you have gaps in your experience and knowledge?

_____

_____

_____

_____

Keep in mind that you want a personal board that supports you and allows you to maintain your independence. What qualities will you seek in the people you look to for advice? Why? How will their characteristics or temperament help you make good decisions and be a strong leader?

_____

_____

_____

_____

Now that you have a clear idea of the kind of advice that could be most beneficial to you, consider who you could tap to provide guidance on those topics and issues. Who can help you see what you might miss? Who can fill the holes in your knowledge? Who has successfully done what you are trying to do?

_____

_____

_____

_____

_____

_____

_____

While you may find it helpful to have people to rely on for advice, you must also be wary. What agendas might these people have? How may their ideals and goals conflict with your own? How could they hold you back?

_____

_____

_____

_____

_____

_____

_____

_____

19

Conclusion: Great Leaders Have Great Outcomes

Great leaders have great outcomes, but all of them get there in different ways. While certain character traits are important, decisions, actions, and results separate the lackluster from the great. Understanding what you do, how you do it, and why you do it can help you develop an organized business model that will help you grow as fast as possible. To keep yourself engaged and on your toes, be conscious and intentional about your decisions and goals.

The following activities will help you remember why you are doing the hard work of leading a fast-growing company.

TRACK YOUR OUTCOMES

Reflect on your responses to the Chapter 1 activities. Consider how your thoughts have expanded or changed as you answer the following questions.

Consider the challenges, rewards, and excitement that are part of your daily life as a leader. What outcomes are you most proud of? What outcomes are you pursuing next?

_____

_____

_____

_____

_____

_____

Which experiences seemed ordinary as they occurred but later revealed themselves to be turning points in your business? What did you learn in those moments?

_____

_____

_____

_____

_____

_____

_____

ORGANIZATIONAL SCAN

Part of being a leader is constantly checking the vital signs in your company. Answer the following questions to get a sense of the work that lies ahead.

What is one way you can raise your standards to energize your people?

_____

_____

What is one way you can better align your people and your organizational culture?

_____

_____

If you were to sharpen your focus on your single most important priority, what would it be?

_____

_____

How can you set the pace to shorten timelines and bring more urgency to your workplace?

_____

_____

Consider your current strategy. How can you transform it to better support your business as it continues to grow?

_____

_____

_____

Index

departmental silos, 67
identification, 67–70
Skills, gaps (filling), 147
Snowflake
 mission, 16
  statement, adaptation, 19
  success, reasons, 16–17
 sales levels (consideration), 33
Solutions, implementation, 77
Spending efficiency, appropriateness, 112
Standards, performer disregard (handling), 62
Strategic transformation
 lead time/foresight, requirement, 137
 preparation, 123–124, 130–131
 progression, identification, 129–130
 timing, 123–124
Strategy
 alternatives, consideration, 36–39
 changes, 41, 133
  communication, 138
 communication, 132
 evolution, defining, 138–140
 execution
  challenges, 139
  sales, impact, 92–93
 execution strategy, summarization, 35
 maximization, ensuring, 129–130
 plans, connection, 129

potential, examination, 129
shift, 138–139
team evaluation, 39–41
vision, alignment, 130
writing, 40, 138–139
Success story, telling/content, 154–155
Super-growers
 factors, 127–128
 potential, identification, 127–128

T
Talents, consideration, 144–145
Team
 appearance/characteristics/behaviors, 48–49
 communication process, 49
 leading, 29–30
 strategy evaluation, 39–41
Technologies, usage, 123
Trust
 absence, 67
 high-trust environment, 72–73

U
Upcoming needs, anticipation/plan, 50
Upselling, sales rep consideration, 95

V
Vision
 clarification, 151
 strategy alignment, 130